India

The Culture and Recipes of India

Tracey Kelly

Power

Published in 2017 by
The Rosen Publishing Group, Inc.
29 East 21st Street, New York, NY 10010

Cataloging-in-Publication Data

Names: Kelly, Tracey.
Title: Culture and recipes of India / Tracey Kelly.
Description: New York : PowerKids Press, 2017. | Series: Let's cook! | Includes index.
Identifiers: ISBN 9781499431797 (pbk.) | ISBN 9781499432596 (library bound) | ISBN 9781499431803 (6 pack)
Subjects: LCSH: Food habits--India--Juvenile literature. | Cooking--India--Juvenile literature.
Classification: LCC TX724.5.I4 K455 2017 |DDC 641.5944--dc23

For Brown Bear Books Ltd:
Text and Editor: Tracey Kelly
Editorial Director: Lindsey Lowe
Children's Publisher: Anne O'Daly
Design Manager: Keith Davis
Designer: Melissa Roskell
Picture Manager: Sophie Mortimer

Picture Credits: t=top, c=center, b=bottom, l=left, r=right. Front Cover: Shutterstock: saiko3p c, pingebat
r, rook76 r, vm2002 r, SMDSS l, D'July l, Noppasin t, milezaway t. Inside: Dreamstime: 17b, 19b, 20-21b, 43;
Shutterstock: 1l, 4, 8-9t, 38-39b, Africa Studio 31t, AJP 5t, Boris B 5br, Hung Chung Chih 7b, CRSHELARE 8,
38-39t, Espies 27b, 33b, 35b, 39, f9photos 6l, 6-7t, HighViews 22b, India Picture 28-29t, Singh Lens 23, Wongyu
Liang 22t, Alexander Mazurkevich 10, Don Mammoser 36-37b, Odua Images 41, RadioKafka 36-37t, Snowbelle 9,
Andrey Starostin 25b, Yuri Taranik 1r, 5b, Aleksander Todorovic 11, Mahathir Mohd Yasin 15b, Katona Zoltan 1bl;
Thinkstock: Geoff Goldswain 30-31, Amit Somvanshi 28-29b, Nathan Soumen 20-21t; Wikipedia: Nauzer 30.

Special thanks to Klaus Arras for all other photography.

Manufactured in the United States of America

CPSIA Compliance Information: Batch #BW17PK: For Further Information contact Rosen Publishing, New York, New York at 1-800-237-9932.

Contents

Let's Cook!

Looking at India

India, in southern Asia, is the world's seventh largest country in area. Over a billion people share its rich culture and history—and its colorful, spicy food!

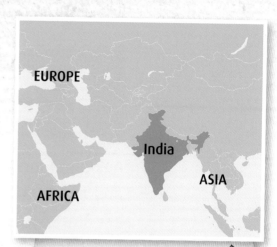

India is bordered by the countries Bangladesh, Nepal, Pakistan, Afghanistan, Sri Lanka, China, and Bhutan.

Cumin   Rosemary

Bay leaves   Chile powder

Saffron   Peppercorns

Jai Hind!

India is a land of contrasts. Around 1.2 billion people make it the second most populated country on Earth, after China. They live in 29 different states with breathtaking landscapes, from snow-covered mountains to vast green plateaus with lush river valleys. Indian religious tradition is deeply spiritual: Hinduism, Buddhism, Jainism, and Sikhism all started here. Sometimes it is as though India is two nations. In rural areas, people live simply, farming the land as they have done for centuries. But in the cities, bustling crowds pack the streets, and many people work for the world's top tech industries. They are all joined together in their love of India's tasty cuisine, though. Jai Hind (Long Live India)!

 Indian cooking uses lots of spices. Common ones include cumin, rosemary, bay leaf, chile, saffron, and pepper.

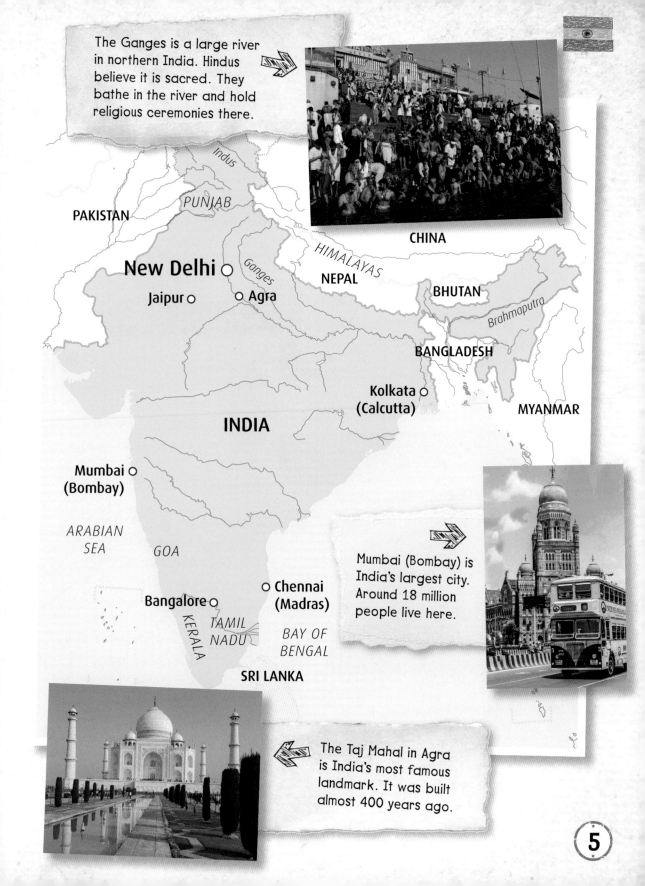

The Ganges is a large river in northern India. Hindus believe it is sacred. They bathe in the river and hold religious ceremonies there.

PAKISTAN

Indus

PUNJAB

New Delhi

Jaipur

Agra

Ganges

HIMALAYAS

NEPAL

CHINA

BHUTAN

Brahmaputra

BANGLADESH

Kolkata
(Calcutta)

MYANMAR

INDIA

Mumbai
(Bombay)

ARABIAN
SEA

GOA

Bangalore

KERALA

TAMIL
NADU

Chennai
(Madras)

BAY OF
BENGAL

SRI LANKA

Mumbai (Bombay) is India's largest city. Around 18 million people live here.

The Taj Mahal in Agra is India's most famous landmark. It was built almost 400 years ago.

South India

The Deccan Plateau makes up most of the southern part of India. This is a huge area of flat lands, or plains. Its altitude (height) goes up to over half a mile (1 kilometer). The plateau has mountain ranges on each side: the Eastern and Western Ghats. The area's hot and humid tropical climate is perfect for growing tea. But this also makes it prone to cyclones, which are fierce tropical storms.

Tea plantations turn the hills a lush green color in Munnar, Kerala, in southern India.

Tso Kar is a saltwater lake in Ladakh, in the Himalayas. It is also called the White Lake because of salt deposits on its shores.

Northern India

Much of the vast Himalayas mountain range stretches across the northern part of India. It has some of the highest mountain peaks on Earth, including Kanchenjunga, which is 28,169 feet (8,586 meters) high. The Himalayas have the largest snow-covered area outside of Earth's polar regions! India's major rivers—the Ganges, Indus, and Brahmaputra—begin to trickle southward as melted water from the glaciers in these mountains.

The Plains

Millions of Indians live in the broad lands of treeless plains south of the Himalayas. The area is very fertile and good for farming because it gets water from the powerful Ganges River. Much of India's food is grown here—and it takes a lot to feed the country's huge population. But the area also is hit with monsoons, heavy rainstorms, in summer and fall.

Built as a British trading fort in the late 1600s, Kolkata is India's second largest city. It is a major port and industrial center. Wealthy people live in grand houses, but nearby, masses of poor people live in run-down slums. In 1950, Catholic missionary Mother Theresa set up the Missionaries of Charity here to help the poor. It is now a worldwide charity.

★ DID YOU KNOW? ★

The official language of India is Hindi, but each state has its own official language, too. Some important languages are: Bengali, Gujarati, Hindi, Kashmiri, Kannada, Konkani, Malayalam, Marathi, Assamese, Punjabi, Sanskrit, and Tamil.

The Victoria Memorial in Kolkata was built in 1901–1926 to honor Queen Victoria. It is a reminder of when Britain ruled India.

Food and Farming

Two-thirds of Indian people work on farms. Many farmers cannot afford time-saving equipment, so the work is done by hand.

Breadbasket

Grains are an important part of the Indian diet. Much of the nation's wheat crops are grown in Punjab, the "breadbasket" of India. The flour is used to make delicious flatbreads called naan, roti, chapati, and paratha. Naan is often flavored with nigella and cumin seeds, and sometimes stuffed with nuts or dried fruit. Wheat is also grown on the plains near the Ganges River, along with rice and corn.

Rice is a very important crop. Grown in the south and the Himalayas, it takes a lot of time and labor to produce. Southern Indians eat it with their meals instead of bread.

A women plants rice seedlings by hand in a rice paddy in Kanchipuram, Tamil Nadu. Rice growing takes a lot of time and effort.

A woman on a small farm tends buffalo. Buffalo and cows are kept for their milk and to make dairy products.

Cattle Call

In rural areas, many farmers keep cattle and buffalo for milk and to make dairy foods, such as yogurt and butter. In fact, India has the largest number of dairy cows in the world—around 45 million! Poor farmers that cannot afford tractors also use cows to pull the plows in the fields. Hindus believe that cows are sacred, so they do not eat their meat.

Legume Land

Legumes, or pulses, are a staple food in India. Many legumes, including different types of lentils, peas, mung beans, pigeon peas, and chickpeas (garbanzo beans), are grown. These foods contain a lot of protein and so are good for a vegetarian diet, which almost a third of Indian people follow. Legumes are fed to cattle, too. They also enrich the soil they are grown in, making it more fertile for the next crop.

Lentils are an important legume in India. They come in red, brown, green, yellow, and black varieties. Chile peppers add heat to food.

Spices of Life

It's hard to think of Indian cuisine without conjuring up the fragrance and taste of spices! Spices have been grown in India for thousands of years. In fact, they were once so valuable that the Portuguese, Dutch, and British took control of India, just so they could trade them.

Today, India is the world's largest producer of spices. The aromatic flavors of aniseed, cardamom, chile, cinnamon, clove, coriander, cumin, garlic, ginger, nutmeg, saffron, and turmeric make Indian dishes taste special. Garam masala (meaning "hot spices") is a common spice blend. Each family has a secret recipe for it. Spices are used as medicines, too, to help digestion or cure a cold, for example. They are also used in cosmetics.

A woman sells colorful spices at a market in Goa. Spices give Indian dishes their unique taste.

Fishermen on the beach drag in nets full of fresh fish from the sea in Kovalam, Kerala.

Fish Tales

With thousands of miles of coastline and many inland lakes and rivers, it's not surprising that fish and other seafood are an important source of food in India. Many Indian dishes, such as curries and pilafs, are based around fish and shrimp. Fishing is also a major industry, and shrimp is exported (sold) to other countries in huge numbers.

Some fisherman have set up cooperatives to share expensive equipment, such as large boats and fishing nets for their catches. They work together in coastal fishing regions, such as the state of Kerala.

DID YOU KNOW?

India is the world's second largest producer of tea, after China. The country grows more than 900,000 tons of tea per year! Tea plants grow well in fairly hot and humid climates, and the northern plains of Assam and Darjeeling produce famous varieties.

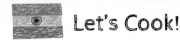
Let's Start Cooking

One thing's for sure—cooking is a lot of fun! In this book, you will learn about different ingredients, which tastes go together, and new cooking methods. Some recipes have steps that you'll need help with, so you can ask a parent or another adult. When your delicious meal is ready, you can serve it to family and friends.

This line tells you how many people the meal will feed.

Serves 4–6

In this box, you find out which ingredients you need for your meal.

YOU WILL NEED

- ✓ 5 ounces milk chocolate or semisweet chocolate (or half of each)
- ✓ 2 large eggs
- ✓ 2 tablespoons confectioner's sugar

Check before you start that you have everything you need. Get all the ingredients ready before you start cooking.

WARNING!

When to Get Help

Most cooking involves chopping ingredients and heating them in some way, whether it's frying, boiling, or baking. Be careful as you cook—and make sure your adult kitchen assistant is around to help!

TOP TIP

You can choose any chocolate you like.

Top Tip gives you more information about the recipe or the ingredients.

For many meals, you need to chop an onion. Cut a thin slice off at both ends, then pull off the papery skin. Cut the onion in half down the middle. Put one half, cut side down, on the cutting board. Hold it with one hand, and cut slices with the other hand. Hold the slices together, then cut across them to make small cubes. Be careful not to cut yourself!

Some recipes use fresh chiles—and they are very hot! Chile seeds and the white pith make your skin burn, so always wear rubber or vinyl gloves when chopping chiles. If you don't have any gloves, wash your hands really well afterward, and do not touch your skin or eyes for a while. To chop, trim the chile stalk, then halve lengthwise. Scrape out the seeds, and throw them away. Slice the stalk into fine pieces.

METRIC CONVERSIONS

Oven Temperature		Liquid		Sugar	
°F	**°C**	**Cups**	**Milliliters**	**Cups**	**Grams**
275	140	¼	60	¼	50
300	150	½	120	½	100
325	170	¾	180	¾	150
350	180	1	240	1	200
375	190				
400	200	**Weight**		**Flour**	
425	220	**Ounces**	**Grams**	**Cups**	**Grams**
450	230	1	30	¼	30
475	240	2	60	½	60
		3	85	¾	90
		4	115	1	120
		5	140		
		6	175		
		7	200		
		8	225		

Garam Masala

Makes 1 jar of spice mix

Every Indian family has their own special recipe for mixing spices. Garam means "hot," and masala means "spices." This is one hot, spicy mix!

YOU WILL NEED

- ✓ 1 tablespoon cardamom pods
- ✓ 1 tablespoon cumin seeds
- ✓ 2 tablespoons coriander seeds
- ✓ 1 tablespoon peppercorns
- ✓ 2 cinnamon sticks
- ✓ 1 teaspoon cloves
- ✓ 1–2 dried chiles
- ✓ ½ teaspoon ground mace

1 Place a skillet on the stove over medium heat without adding any fat.

2 Now add the cardamom pods, cumin and coriander seeds, peppercorns, cinnamon sticks, cloves, and chiles.

3 Dry-roast the spices for a few minutes. Using a wooden spoon, stir them so that they don't burn.

4 Let the spices cool for a few minutes. Then crush them with a pestle and mortar. Or you can grind them in a spice mill. Stir in the mace.

5 Spoon the garam masala into a clean jar or container with a tight lid. Keep the spice mix in a cool, dark place, and it will last for several weeks.

TOP TIP

Garam masala is used to flavor savory Indian dishes. It can be added at the beginning of cooking, or you can sprinkle it in when the dish is almost cooked.

Lentil Dal

Serves 4

A dal is a stew made from legumes, such as lentils. It comes from southern India, where many people are vegetarians (people who don't eat meat).

YOU WILL NEED

- ✔ 10 ounces yellow split lentils
- ✔ salt, black pepper
- ✔ 1 bunch scallions
- ✔ 1 red and 1 green bell pepper
- ✔ 3 garlic cloves
- ✔ 3 red chiles
- ✔ 2 tablespoons ghee (clarified butter) or cooking oil
- ✔ 1 teaspoon each of garam masala (see pages 14–15), turmeric, coriander seeds, and ground cumin

1 In a colander, rinse the lentils with water. Then pick out any that look a different color or are empty shells.

DID YOU KNOW?

The word dal means "split pulses," especially lentils. India is the world's biggest consumer of pulses, or legumes!

2 Put the good lentils in a saucepan, and add 2½ cups of cold water. Add ½ teaspoon salt, and grind in lots of pepper. Bring to a boil. Put the lid on the pan, and reduce the heat to low. Simmer for about 25 minutes. The lentils should be cooked but not too soft.

3 Now wash and trim the vegetables. Slice the scallions into thin rings, and cut the bell peppers into thin strips.

4 Peel and finely chop the garlic. Trim, deseed, and chop the chiles (see page 13).

5 In a wide skillet, heat the ghee or cooking oil. Add the scallion, pepper, garlic, and chiles. Fry for about 2 minutes, stirring all the time.

6 Now add the spices, and fry for a few seconds. Spoon in the lentils with their juices. Stir, and heat again. Season with salt and pepper, and serve.

chapatis

Makes 12

Lots of different yummy breads are baked in India! There are chapatis, parathas, naans, and rotis. Much of the wheat is grown in the north.

YOU WILL NEED

- ✓ 3/4 pound atta flour
- ✓ 1 tablespoon salt
- ✓ 1 tablespoon cooking oil
- ✓ 1 cup lukewarm water

1 Put the flour and salt in a bowl, and mix. Add the oil, then the water. Knead it to make a smooth dough.

2 Let the dough rest at room temperature for 2 hours.

3 Divide the dough into 12 equal chunks, and shape each into a ball.

4 Flour a work surface, then roll out each ball to make a circle about 4 inches (10 cm) wide.

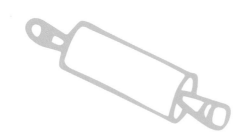

TOP TIP

Atta is an Indian flour made from hard, stone-ground durum wheat. If you can't find it at the grocery store, use whole wheat flour instead.

5 Add a thin dusting of flour to the circles, so that they don't stick together. Now pile them up on top of each other.

6 Heat a cast-iron skillet without oil. When it's hot, add the dough circles, one at a time. Cook for a few seconds on each side. They are cooked when they puff up and show brown spots.

7 When the chapatis are all done, put them in a basket or on a plate. Wrap a clean cloth around them to keep the chapatis warm.

Let's Cook!

National
Festivals

Indian people celebrate lots of festivals! Some honor gods and goddesses, the changing seasons, or myths. Some celebrate political events. Each is marked with shows, rituals, and delicious foods.

Indian Independence

People celebrate Indian Independence Day on August 15. On this day in 1947, the nation gained freedom from British rule after almost 200 years. To show respect, the Indian flag is raised in public places. Children sing songs at school and are given candies. Family and friends gather for lunch or dinner, just as they do on US Independence Day. Kite-flying competitions are also popular.

On October 2, India celebrates Gandhi Jayanti, a holiday that honors Mahatma Gandhi. Gandhi was a great political and spiritual leader who helped India gain its freedom. He did this by using nonviolent methods to spread his message. People all around the world were inspired by him. Sadly, he was assassinated (killed) shortly after the new Indian government was set up.

A group of children celebrate Indian Independence Day. They have fun dancing beneath the flag of India.

This girl is making a Rangoli, a decoration of patterns using colored ground rice. The design is lit with oil lamps called diyas.

Divine Diwali

India's most important holiday is Diwali, the Hindu festival of light. Held for five days in the fall, it celebrates the symbolic victory of light over darkness. Diwali also honors the goddess Lakshmi, who represents prosperity (success). People pray to her to send them good luck for the coming year. In the past, Diwali was celebrated only by Hindu, Sikh, and Jain people. But the holiday is so enjoyable that today, everyone in the country celebrates!

People clean their homes and give each other gifts to usher in Diwali. They light candles and clay lamps called diyas to symbolize the triumph of light. Amazing fireworks are set off into the skies. Indians also prepare large feasts by making special dishes. A Diwali dessert called burfi is made from condensed milk and sugar. Sometimes rosewater and almonds are added.

DID YOU KNOW?

Rangoli is a type of folk art that is used during Indian festivals and holidays. Bright designs are made in rice flour, colored sand, or flower petals. They are placed on the floor near the door of homes to welcome visitors—including the goddess Lakshmi!

Eid ul-Fitr

About 14 percent of Indians are Muslims, the second largest religious group in India. The most important Muslim celebration is called Eid ul-Fitr, which comes at the end of the month of Ramadan. This is a time when people follow a strict fast to develop self-control. They pray and read the Koran every day. By the end of Ramadan, people are ready for a big feast! The Eid ul-Fitr festivities start when the new moon first appears in the sky. Muslims pray together and give money to the poor. Then they dress up, go to local celebrations, and prepare a feast. Delicious dishes are made, such as chicken and rosewater biryani.

A mother and her two daughters prepare food for a meal that will end the Ramadan fast.

Pretty sweets made with milk, nuts, and fruits are traditional at Eid ul-Fitr.

The faces of these young men are decorated with colored powders to celebrate Holi.

Colorful Holi

Holi, or the "Festival of Colors," is a Hindu celebration that marks the arrival of spring. It happens in March, just as green leaves appear on the trees and colorful flowers begin to bloom. People light bonfires and throw chickpeas and popcorn on them. The next day, people come out into the streets, dancing and singing. Crowds of all ages throw colored powders on each other—they try to become as brightly colored as possible to mimic the springtime colors. Some people think Holi began when the young Hindu god, Krishna, threw colored water at some milkmaids as a practical joke. He was a high-spirited god!

DID YOU KNOW?

During festivals, candies are sometimes decorated with edible silver or gold leaf to make them look really special.

Vegetable Curry

Serves 4

This delicious dish is eaten during the festival of Diwali. The variety of vegetables symbolizes having enough to eat all year round.

YOU WILL NEED

- ✓ 2/3 cup dried black-eyed peas, soaked in water overnight
- ✓ 1 onion
- ✓ 2 garlic cloves
- ✓ 1-inch piece fresh ginger
- ✓ 1½ pounds vegetables (as many different kinds as possible; for example, baby corncobs, carrots, green beans, cauliflower, tomatoes)
- ✓ 3 tablespoons cooking oil
- ✓ 1–2 tablespoons garam masala
- ✓ about 1¼ cups hot water
- ✓ salt, black pepper
- ✓ 2 tablespoons fresh cilantro leaves

1 Rinse the black-eyed peas in plenty of water. Put them into a saucepan, and cover with cold water. Bring to a boil, then drain in a colander. Rinse again in cold running water.

2 Put the black-eyed peas back in the saucepan and cover with water. Bring to a boil again. Turn down the heat, cover, and simmer over low heat for 50 minutes until they are almost soft. Look at them every 10 minutes. Add a little more water if they start to look dry.

4 Put the oil in a deep, wide saucepan, and heat slowly. Add the onion, garlic, and ginger. Fry for a few minutes, until they turn golden yellow.

5 Add the vegetables to the pan in small batches, starting with the hardest. Fry and stir for 2 minutes, then add another batch. When all the vegetables have been added, sprinkle with garam masala, then fry for 1 minute. Finally, add the hot water, and stir.

3 Next, peel the onion, garlic, and ginger. Chop the onion and the ginger into little chunks. Crush the garlic. Wash and trim the other vegetables. Now cut the vegetables into bite-size pieces.

6 Drain the black-eyed peas, and add them to the vegetables. Stir, cover the pan, and simmer over low heat for 15 minutes. Season with salt and pepper. Scatter with cilantro leaves, and serve.

DID YOU KNOW?

Black-eyed peas are also called cowpeas. They have a lot of protein, so they are a good food for vegetarians.

Seviyan

Serves 6–8

This sweet and yummy dessert is made with milk and noodles. It is served at the Eid ul-Fitr feast at the end of Ramadan, after people have fasted.

YOU WILL NEED

- ✓ 1 teaspoon green cardamom pods
- ✓ 1 tablespoon ghee or cooking oil
- ✓ 7 cups milk
- ✓ 4 ounces seviyan (thin vermicelli noodles from India or Pakistan)
- ✓ 1 tablespoon chopped almonds
- ✓ 1 tablespoon finely chopped pistachio nuts
- ✓ 2 tablespoons raisins
- ✓ ½ cup sugar
- ✓ 4/5 cup cream

1 Pop open the cardamom pods. Push out all the green seeds, then carefully chop the seeds with a knife.

DID YOU KNOW?

Ghee is clarified butter made from buffalo or cow's milk. It is made by simmering butter until the water evaporates. Grocery stores sell it in the ethnic food section.

2 Put the ghee or cooking oil in a saucepan and heat over low heat. Add the cardamom seeds, and fry them for a few seconds. Put the milk in another pan, and heat (don't let it boil!).

3 Break the noodles into smaller pieces, then add to the pan with the ghee and cardamom. Fry them for a few minutes over medium heat. They should turn a light brown color.

4 Add the hot milk and bring to a boil. Turn down the heat and simmer for 5 minutes. Keep stirring all the time so that the milk doesn't burn.

5 Stir in the almonds, pistachios, and raisins. Let everything simmer for about 15 minutes, until the mixture has thickened a little. Keep stirring every few minutes so it doesn't stick to the bottom.

6 Take the saucepan off the heat. Stir in the sugar and cream. Decorate with some extra nuts. The seviyan thickens as it cools, and you can serve hot or cold.

Celebrating at Home

Family life is cherished in India. Celebrations for birthdays and life-cycle rituals called samskaras involve the entire family. Weddings are even bigger celebrations!

Happy Birthdays

Birthdays are huge celebrations in India, bigger than Christmas! Hindu children go to school on their birthday dressed from head to foot in a brand-new outfit. They wear bright, colorful new clothes, new shoes, and new accessories, such as bracelets and hair ribbons. At school, children bring candies to hand out to classmates and teachers. Everyone sings "Happy Birthday" on their special day.

At home, a blessing is given to the birthday boy or girl. The whole family gathers to share a large meal at dinnertime. This will include the birthday person's favorite dish, such as coconut pilaf, and side dishes. A big birthday cake is lit with candles and shared. Later, after the guests leave, the birthday person opens his or her gifts.

Two girls blow out the candles on a big birthday cake. Birthdays are a time of joy and family celebration in India.

A woman ties a rakhi bracelet on her brother's hand as a token of sisterly love during a Raksha Bandan celebration.

Sibling Rakhi

A Hindu festival called Raksha Bandan takes place in August. This is the celebration of the love and care shared between a sister and her brother or male cousin. It can also be between a sister and someone she considers her brother, such as a family friend.

The sister and brother gather with the family, and she paints a tilak, a decoration, on his forehead. She then ties a rakhi, a braided bracelet, around his wrist. This symbolizes her love and prayers for his life and happiness, and she places a candy in his mouth. The brother then promises that he will always protect his sister and gives her his blessing. He gives her a gift of money or jewelry, too.

★ DID YOU KNOW?

A tilak is a mark, often a dot, painted on a someone's forehead. It can be a line or other shapes, too. Sometimes it tells what caste (class) a person belongs to. On a woman, it can also be a sign that she is married. ★

Life-Cycle Rituals

In the Hindu religion, a set of 16 rituals called samskaras mark different stages in a person's life. There are rituals to mark things like the birth of a baby, when it is named, or when it goes outside for the first time.

Another samskara marks the day that a child first goes to school and starts to gain knowledge. Girls and boys have different growing-up samskara rituals, such as when a boy first shaves his face or when a girl blossoms into womanhood. Marriage is another important ritual. The last samskara is a ritual performed when a person dies.

A couple celebrates the annaprashan samskara, which marks their baby's first taste of solid food.

This young woman has a henna tattoo called a mehndi on her hands.

An Indian couple prays at their traditional wedding ceremony. The bride wears a bright pink and red sari.

Wedding Samskara

Marriage is an important step in a person's life. In India, parents often choose a life partner for their son or daughter. This is called an arranged marriage. People believe that not only do the bride and groom marry, but their families do, too. The wedding lasts several days, so the families can get to know each other at festive meals and parties.

There are many marriage customs. Before the wedding, the bride is decorated with mehndi, beautiful henna tattoos. The groom often rides to the ceremony on a white horse! The couple then puts floral garlands on each other to show their love. Under a *mandap* (canopy), they say their marriage vows with a priest around a sacred fire.

DID YOU KNOW?

The wedding mehndi custom goes back 5,000 years. But it came into fashion for all in the late 1990s. Stars like Beyoncé have worn mehndi tattoos. Modern versions even use glitter!

Tandoori Chicken

Serves 4

People eat this flavorful Indian chicken dish on special occasions. Traditionally, it is cooked over charcoal in a clay oven called a tandoor.

YOU WILL NEED

- 2 garlic cloves
- 2-inch piece fresh ginger
- 4 teaspoons tandoori spice mix
- ½ cup low-fat yogurt
- 4 chicken legs
- 2 whole chicken breasts with bones
- cooking oil for brushing
- salt

PLUS:

- lettuce
- juice of 1 lemon
- 2 teaspoons ground cumin
- 2 onions, cut into slices
- fresh mint leaves, to garnish
- yogurt dip, to serve

1 Peel the garlic and ginger piece. Chop finely, and put into a big bowl. Add the tandoori spices and yogurt, and stir well to mix.

2 Add the chicken legs and breasts to the bowl. Brush the pieces with the yogurt mix, then cover the bowl. Chill in the refrigerator overnight or for 12 hours.

4 Using tongs, turn each chicken piece over. Brush them with a little oil, and sprinkle with salt. Bake for another 20 minutes in the oven.

5 Put lettuce leaves on a platter, and add the cooked chicken. Drizzle with lemon juice and sprinkle with cumin. Add onion slices, and garnish with mint leaves. Serve with yogurt dip.

3 Preheat the oven to 450°F. One by one, take the chicken pieces out of the yogurt sauce, and pat them dry with paper towels. Place them on a rack, and bake in the oven for 20 minutes.

DID YOU KNOW?

The spices that go into tandoori seasoning include ginger, nutmeg, paprika, cardamom, cinnamon, cloves, coriander, cumin, turmeric, and pepper.

SAFETY TIP

Always wash your hands with soap and warm water after handling raw chicken. Wash all cutting boards and utensils used to prepare raw chicken, too.

Vegetable Samosas

Makes 16–20

Samosas are a tasty and healthy snack! They can be made with different fillings and are delicious dipped in fruit chutney or a spicy dip.

YOU WILL NEED

FOR THE PASTRY:
- 3½ tablespoons ghee or oil
- 2 cups all-purpose flour
- 1 teaspoon salt
- 1 teaspoon lemon juice

FOR THE FILLING:
- 7 ounces potatoes
- 1/4 cauliflower
- 1 small zucchini
- 2 tablespoons ghee or cooking oil, plus extra for frying
- 2 teaspoons garam masala
- 1 teaspoon ground ginger
- ½ teaspoon turmeric
- 1 teaspoon cayenne
- ½ teaspoon ground cumin
- salt

1 Over low heat, melt the ghee. Mix it with the flour, ½ cup lukewarm water, salt, and lemon juice. To make a smooth dough, knead for about 10 minutes. Wrap the dough in plastic wrap to keep it moist, then let it rest for 30 minutes.

2 To make the filling, peel the potatoes and cut into cubes. Wash, trim, and cube the cauliflower and zucchini. Heat the ghee or oil in a saucepan. Add the vegetables, fry, and stir for 2 minutes. Now add the spices and salt. Fry and stir for 1 minute. Pour in ½ cup water, and cover the saucepan. Turn down the heat, and simmer for 10 minutes. Take off the lid, and simmer until the liquid is gone.

DID YOU KNOW?

Samosas can be filled with lots of different vegetables. In India, they often have a potato and pea filling with cashews.

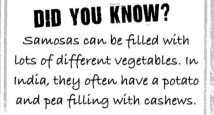

3 Knead the dough once more, then roll it out in small sheets. Put a plate 8 inches (20 cm) in diameter on top of the dough. Cut a circle around it. Knead the leftover dough pieces, then roll them out again, and cut more circles.

4 Cut each circle in half, and put 1 heaped teaspoon of filling in the middle of each. Wet the edges with a little water. Now fold one corner on top of the other, and squeeze the straight and the round edges together.

5 In a skillet, heat the remaining ghee or oil. Fry the samosas, a few at a time, for about 2 minutes. Turn carefully, and fry for 2 more minutes. Lift them out with a slotted spoon onto paper towels. Serve with onions slices and dips.

Daily Life in India

India's huge, sprawling cities are fueled by modern science and industry. But in its rural areas, people still live very simply in traditional ways.

Urban Life

India's major cities are teeming with millions of people. Wealthy homes lie just down the street from run-down slums where people live in extreme poverty. In Mumbai, cars, textiles, and machinery are manufactured, employing lots of people. Delhi, India's capital, is a major business center. Young people here work in well-paid jobs at call centers for companies in other countries. Kolkata is a big industrial city and port, but it is also home to thousands of street children.

People walk through Chawri Bazar, a busy market that sells metal and paper products. Delhi is a crowded city of almost 10 million people.

People buy vegetables and fruit at simple local markets. These markets are common all across India.

Rural Ways

Around two-thirds of Indian people live in small villages in the countryside. Families farm small plots of land to grow food for themselves. Most of it is done by hand, so the work is very hard. Sometimes children cannot go to school because they are needed to help grow and harvest crops. Any extra foods are taken to the local markets and sold.

Some villages have electricity, but many still don't have running water. Women walk to wells and carry water home in buckets. They wash clothes in rivers and streams. Where there are no sewage facilities, diseases can spread easily as human waste gets into the ground and rivers.

DID YOU KNOW?

Indian Railways runs one of the biggest and busiest railroad networks in the world. It employs 1.3 million people, making it one of the largest employers in the world, too.

37

Many families cannot afford enough food. These schoolchildren in Dharni have been given a free lunch.

School Days

In India, children between the ages of 6 and 14 can attend state schools for free. First, they go to lower primary (age 6 to 10) and upper primary school (age 10 to 14). They then attend high school (age 14 to 18), which is split into secondary and higher secondary school.

Private schools with low-cost tuition have become popular in India. Many poor families scrape together the money to send their children to them, because children will receive a better education. And if children are well-educated, they have a chance to find better jobs and escape poverty. Students study hard to get good grades!

★ DID YOU KNOW?

More movies are made in India than anywhere else in the world. Bollywood is part of the movie industry based in Mumbai (Bombay). The name takes the "B" from "Bombay" and the rest from "Hollywood." ★

All in the Family

Extended families often live together in India. So parents, siblings, grandparents, uncles, aunts, and cousins may all share one home! This is easier in the country, where houses have more room. But in cities, homes are smaller, and it's not always possible to live in one place.

Meals offer families a chance to spend quality time together. Delicious foods made with fragrant spices are always prepared fresh. Popular dishes include lentil dal or a thali, a tray with rice, chapatis, chutney, and a vegetable curry or rogan josh.

A thali tray contains a selection of curries, chutneys, and breads, made to be eaten with the hands.

This Bollywood actor wears bright, colorful clothes. Bollywood movies feature lots of dancing and singing!

Time to Relax

Bollywood movies are a popular way for people to relax after work or school. They are full of adventure, romance, singing, and dancing. People also listen to music, such as Indian classical or bhangra, which mixes Punjabi folk with Western pop music. Sports are very popular, too, especially cricket. Indians follow their favorite teams and play themselves whenever they can.

Cool Lassi

Makes 6–8 glasses

Try this chilled yogurt drink on a hot day! Lassi also helps cool your mouth if you are eating hot and spicy food.

YOU WILL NEED

- ✓ 1 cup whole-milk yogurt
- ✓ 1 cup chilled water
- ✓ salt
- ✓ ½ teaspoon ground cumin
- ✓ 1 teaspoon lemon juice
- ✓ crushed ice
- ✓ some fresh mint leaves

1 Put the yogurt, chilled water, salt, ground cumin, and lemon juice into a measuring cup or bowl.

2 Mix all the ingredients with a spoon or a whisk to combine. Stir them well to make a smooth, icy drink.

TOP TIP

Use an ice crusher to crush the ice cubes. Or, put the cubes in a plastic bag, wrap in a towel, and pound with a rolling pin.

3 Half-fill the glasses with crushed ice, then pour the lassi on top. Decorate the drinks with fresh mint leaves, and serve.

TOP TIP

Mango lassis are easy to make. Mash the flesh of 1 mango with 4 cups whole-milk yogurt, 1 cup chilled water, and 4 tablespoons sugar. Put crushed ice into glasses, and add the lassi.

Rogan Josh

Serves 4

This dish is a classic North Indian favorite. Every family has its own "secret" recipe! Rogan Josh tastes great served with basmati rice.

YOU WILL NEED

- ✓ 2 pounds lamb (from the leg)
- ✓ ½-inch piece ginger
- ✓ 3 garlic cloves
- ✓ 2 onions
- ✓ 5 tablespoons ghee or oil
- ✓ ½ cup whole-milk yogurt
- ✓ salt
- ✓ fresh cilantro leaves

FOR THE SPICE MIXTURE:
- ✓ ½ teaspoon ground cardamom
- ✓ a pinch of ground cloves
- ✓ ½ teaspoon ground black pepper
- ✓ a pinch of ground cinnamon
- ✓ 1 teaspoon hot paprika
- ✓ 1 teaspoon ground coriander
- ✓ 1 teaspoon ground cumin

1 Using a clean cutting board and a sharp knife, cut the lamb into bite-size chunks.

DID YOU KNOW?

Rogan josh is traditionally made with mutton, a meat that comes from an older sheep than lamb. It has a stronger flavor and needs to be stewed for a long time.

2 Peel the ginger, garlic, and onions, and chop them into small pieces. Mix the spice mixture in a small bowl.

3 Put the ghee or oil in a large saucepan, and heat. Add the meat chunks and fry them all over, stirring, until they no longer look pink.

4 Remove the meat and set it aside. Now add the garlic, onions, and ginger. Fry for 2 minutes. Add the spice mixture, stir, and fry for 2 more minutes.

5 Put the meat back in the saucepan. Add the yogurt, 1 cup water, and 1 teaspoon salt, and stir. Simmer for 1 hour over low heat.

6 Every 10 minutes or so, stir the curry, adding more water if it gets too dry. Scatter fresh cilantro on top, and serve with cooked basmati rice.

Coconut Pilaf

Serves 4

This flavorful recipe from Kerala is often made as a vegetarian dish. Here, shrimp or chicken is added. Coconut milk brings the flavors together.

YOU WILL NEED

- 2 cups basmati rice
- salt
- 4 garlic cloves
- 2-inch piece fresh ginger
- 1–2 chiles
- 2 teaspoons ground cumin
- 1 teaspoon ground cardamom
- a pinch of ground cinnamon
- 1 large onion
- 2 tablespoons cooking oil
- 3 tomatoes
- ½ cup full-fat yogurt
- ½ cup unsweetened coconut milk
- 3/4 pound peeled cooked shrimp (or cubed chicken)
- 2 tablespoons cashews, chopped and roasted
- a handful of scallion slices

1 Rinse the rice in a colander. Put it in a saucepan with 2½ cups of cold water and 1 teaspoon salt. Bring to a boil, stir, and cover. Simmer the rice over low heat for 15–20 minutes. If it looks dry, add a little more water.

2 Next, peel the garlic and ginger. Trim and deseed the chiles (see page 13). Put garlic, ginger, chiles, cumin, cardamom, and cinnamon into a cup with 3 tablespoons water. Puree in the mixer until it becomes a fairly smooth paste.

3 Peel and chop the onion. In a deep skillet, heat the oil, add the onion, and fry until it is golden brown. Chop the tomatoes.

5 Add in the rice, and season with a little salt. Scatter the roasted cashews and scallions across the top of the dish, and serve.

4 Add the spice paste, and stir well. Using a wooden spoon, stir in the tomatoes, yogurt, and coconut milk. Cook over medium heat for 10 minutes, stirring occasionally. Add the shrimp, and cook for 3–4 minutes.

DID YOU KNOW?

"Pilaf" is originally a Persian word. There are different spellings: pilau, pilav, pulao. The main ingredient in pilaf is usually chicken or seafood. Nuts, coconut, and dried fruits are often added, too.

Glossary

chapati One of many different types of bread in India.

chutney A condiment made from fruit or vegetables, spices, vinegar, and sugar.

dal (1) A legume; a dried split bean or pea; (2) a stewlike dish made from legumes.

Diwali The Hindu Festival of Light, one of the biggest Indian celebrations.

garam masala A spice mix; the words mean "hot spices." It is often sprinkled on a dish at the end of cooking.

ghee Clarified butter used in Indian cooking.

henna The powdered leaves of a shrub used to make mehndi (a temporary tattoo) or hair dye.

Holi A festival marking springtime; people throw colored powders and paints on each other.

mehndi (1) A temporary tattoo, applied to the hands and feet, especially before a wedding; (2) the party at which wedding tattoos are applied.

lassi A popular drink made with yogurt or buttermilk.

legumes Also known as pulses, these are shelled and split beans or peas commonly used in Indian cooking.

samosa A deep-fried pastry triangle filled with vegetables or meat.

samskara A life-cycle celebration, such as a birth, name-giving, first day of school, or a wedding.

seviyan A sweet dessert dish eaten or given for the Muslim festival of Ramadan Eid ul-Fitr.

tandoor A clay oven that reaches a high temperature and is used for cooking meat dishes, such as tandoori chicken, and different breads.

tandoori spice mix A reddish-yellow spice mixture used to marinate chicken or other dishes before cooking in the tandoor oven.

thali A silver tray used to hold several different Indian dishes, such as curries and dals, with chutneys, rice, and pieces of bread.

Further Resources

Books

Aloian, Molly.
Cultural Traditions in India (Cultural Traditions in My World).
Crabtree Publishing, New York: 2012.

Brooks, Susie.
India (The Land and the People).
Gareth Stevens, New York: 2016.

DK editors.
Gandhi (Eyewitness).
DK Children's Books, New York: 2014.

Ejaz, Khadija.
We Visit India (Your Land and My Land: Asia).
Mitchell Lane Publishers, Hockessin, DE: 2014.

Ganeri, Anita.
Indian Culture (Global Cultures).
Heinneman, Portsmouth, NH: 2012.

Glossop, Jennifer.
The Kids Book of World Religions.
Kids Can Press, Toronto: 2013.

Websites

Due to the changing nature of Internet links, PowerKids Press has developed an online list of websites related to the subject of this book. This site is updated regularly. Please use this link to access the list:

www.powerkidslinks.com/lc/india

Index